Wildflowers

Wildflowers

A GARDEN PRIMER

Anne Velghe

Farrar Straus Giroux   New York

A maman et à Moune

6

SNOWDROP
Galanthus nivalis

Among the first of the spring flowers, the snowdrop symbolizes consolation, perhaps because it is evidence that winter will soon give way to spring. It has also been called "Fair Maids of February."

COLTSFOOT
Tussilago farfara

The coltsfoot is so named because its leaf is said to resemble a horse's hoof. An extract of the leaves makes a good cough remedy, hence its other name, *tussilago*, from the Latin *tussis*, "cough."

DAISY
Bellis perennis

For its habit of opening and closing its petals morning and evening, the flower was originally called Day's Eye, which became *daisy*. The buds are often pink, and turn white as they mature.

DRAGONFLY
order *Odonata*

Dragonfly fossils—some with two-foot wingspans—have been found dating back to the Paleozoic era. Highly sensitive to light, dragonflies live near ponds and streams, and are extremely helpful in controlling mosquitoes.

DANDELION
Taraxacum officinale

The young greens of the dandelion are now commonly used in salads, but they were also used by herbalists (the *officinale* in its name) as a diuretic and a cathartic. The word *dandelion* comes from the French *dent de lion*, "lion's tooth." Scattering with one breath the plant's balloon of silver seeds—the bane of all gardeners—is thought to solve the perennial dilemma "He loves me, he loves me not."

9

10

11

12

13

14

POPPY
Papaver rhoeas

Many battlefields of World War I were covered with these beautiful scarlet flowers before and after the war. Now a poppy worn in the lapel on Veterans (or Armistice) Day commemorates those lost in war.

CHICORY
Cichorium intybus

Although the beautiful blue flowers of the chicory plant last only a single day each, the roots have been used for centuries as a coffee substitute or additive.

LADYBUG
family *Coccinellidae*

There are about 3,000 species of ladybug (more than 400 in North America alone), and their usefulness as an environmentally friendly method of pest control has made them the farmer's and the gardener's friend.

STRAWBERRY
Fragaria vesca

This wild form of the strawberry produces a slightly smaller but even sweeter berry. With its lovely white flowers, deep green leaves, and delicious fruit, this plant has something to please everyone and understandably epitomizes "perfect excellence."

DOG ROSE
Rosa canina

Though the leaves of this species of wild rose have no odor, the flowers are wonderfully perfumed. The dog rose's more common cousin, rugosa (wrinkled) rose, is currently being planted along some seashores to prevent beach erosion.

20

21

BROOM
Cytisus scoparius

In the fourteenth century, Geoffrey, Count of Anjou, was fond of wearing a sprig of broom—then called *planta genista*—in his cap. This led to his nickname, Plantagenet, which became the name of an English royal family.

FOXGLOVE
Digitalis purpurea

Like many wildflowers, foxglove can both harm and help. The entire plant contains the toxin *digitalis glycosides*, which is highly poisonous if eaten. The purple, or *purpurea*, species is the most toxic. Foxglove is also the source of the medication digitalin, used since 1800 to treat heart ailments.

FROGS
family *Ranidae*

Besides providing other benefits, frogs are important in controlling the insect population. However, their number and variety have diminished drastically in recent years, wherever the land and water have been contaminated. If you see or hear frogs, the land is healthy.

HONEYSUCKLE
Lonicera japonica

Although considered a pest in some areas because its prodigious growth (sometimes up to thirty feet a year) crowds out other plants, the honeysuckle has a heavenly scent. Its flowers, picked early, can be used for potpourri.

TANSY
Tanacetum vulgare

A member of the sunflower family, the tansy has had its place at meals during both Passover and Lent. Now, however, it is known that this bitter-tasting plant contains a toxic oil and should not be eaten. After being hung upside down to dry, the buttonlike flowers make a wonderful, long-lasting decoration.

28

29

30

31

1
SNOWDROP
Galanthus nivalis
(Amaryllis family)

4 to 5 inches
March to April
—Consolation

2
COLTSFOOT
Tussilago farfara
(Sunflower family)

3 to 18 inches
March to June

3
WOOD ANEMONE
Anemone nemorosa
(Buttercup family)

6 inches
April to June
—Forlornness

4
DOG VIOLET
Viola conspersa
(Violet family)

3 to 8 inches
March to June
—Love

5
EVENING PRIMROSE
Oenothera biennis
(Evening Primrose family)

2 to 5 feet
June to September
—Inconstancy

6
FORGET-ME-NOT
Myosotis sylvatica
(Forget-me-not family)

6 to 24 inches
May to October
—Remembrance, true love

7
DAISY
Bellis perennis
(Sunflower family)

1 to 2 feet
May to September
—Innocence

8
BUTTERCUP
Ranunculus acris
(Buttercup family)

2 to 3 feet
May to September
—Cheerfulness, childishness

9
DANDELION
Taraxacum officinale
(Sunflower family)

2 to 18 inches
March to September

10
POPPY
Papaver rhoeas
(Poppy family)

5 inches to 4 feet
May to July
—Consolation

11
CHICORY
Cichorium intybus
(Sunflower family)

1 to 4 feet
June to October

12
SPEEDWELL
Veronica officinalis
(Snapdragon family)

3 to 10 inches
May to July
—Fidelity

13
OXEYE DAISY
Chrysanthemum leucanthemum
(Sunflower family)

1 to 3 feet
June to August
—A token

14
MEADOW QUEEN
Filipendula ulmaria
(Rose family)

2 to 3 feet
June to August

15
RASPBERRY
Rubus idaeus
(Rose family)

Shrub
June to September
—Remorse

16
BLACKBERRY
Rubus caesius
(Rose family)

Shrub
July to August

17
WILD STRAWBERRIES
Fragaria vesca
(Rose family)

3 to 6 inches
May to August
—Perfect excellence

18
ZIGZAG CLOVER
Trifolium medium
(Pea family)

6 to 24 inches
May to September
—Industry

19
DOG ROSE
Rosa canina
(Rose family)

4 to 6 feet
June to September
—Pleasure and pain

20
HAREBELL
Campanula rotundifolia
(Bluebell family)

6 to 20 inches
June to September

21
BROOM
Cytisus scoparius
(Pea family)

3 to 5 feet
May to June
—Neatness

22
ELDERBERRY
Sambucus canadensis
(Honeysuckle family)

3 to 12 feet
June to July

23
BULL THISTLE
Cirsium vulgare
(Sunflower family)

2 to 6 feet
June to September
—Austerity

24
TEASEL
Dipsacus sylvestris
(Teasel family)

2 to 6 feet
July to October

25
FIREWEED
Epilobium angustifolium
(Evening Primrose family)

2 to 6 feet
July to September

26
FOXGLOVE
Digitalis purpurea
(Snapdragon family)

1 to 7 feet
May to July
—Insincerity

27
HEDGE BINDWEED
Convolvulus sepium
(Morning Glory family)

3 to 10 feet (vine)
May to September
—Insinuation

28
STINGING NETTLE
Urtica dioica
(Nettle family)

2 to 4 feet
June to September
—Slander

29
HONEYSUCKLE
Lonicera japonica
(Honeysuckle family)

Creeping vine
April to July
—Inconstancy

30
TANSY
Tanacetum vulgare
(Sunflower family)

2 to 3 feet
July to September

31
WILD CHERVIL or HONEWORT
Anthriscus cerefolium
(Parsley family)

1 to 3 feet
June to September

32
COW PARSNIP
or HOGWEED
Heracleum lanatum
(Parsley family)

4 to 9 feet
June to August

Published simultaneously in Canada by HarperCollins*Canada*Ltd
Library of Congress catalog card number: 93-73032
Printed and bound in Belgium
First American edition, 1994